YOUNG EXPLORER SERIES

BATS

VAMPIRE
BATS...

KIMBERLY J. WILLIAMS
ERIK D. STOOPS

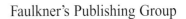

Faulkner's Publishing Group

Dedicated to Susan Barnard of Basically Bats for help with my first vampire bat baby, Vodoo.

Library of Congress Cataloging-in-Publication Data

Williams, Kim, 1966-
    Vampire bats-- / Kimberly Joan Williams, Erik Daniel Stoops.
      p. cm. -- (Young explorers series. Bats)
    ISBN 1-890475-17-3
     1. Vampire bats--Juvenile literature. I.Stoops, Erik D., 1966- II. Title.

  QL737.C52 W56 2000   00-047627

First published in North America in 2001 by
Faulkner's Publishing Group, Inc.
200 Paw Paw Ave #124
Benton Harbor, MI 49022

This edition © 2001 by Faulkner's Publishing Group, Inc.
Text by Kimberly Joan Williams and Erik Daniel Stoops
Photographs © 2001 by Kimberly J. Williams, John Seyjaget, Earl A. Robinson, and Rob Mies.

Text: Kimberly Joan Williams and Erik Daniel Stoops
Page Layout: Rebecca A. Haas-Preuss
Cover Design: Rebecca A. Haas-Preuss

Printed in the United States of America

1 2 3 4 5 6 7 8 9 03 02 01 00 99

Table of Contents

CHAPTER ONE Bat Basics ....**PAGES 4-9**

CHAPTER TWO Eating Habits of Vampire Bats ....**PAGES 10-15**

CHAPTER THREE Habitats of Vampire Bats ....**PAGES 16-17**

CHAPTER FOUR Baby Vampire Bats ....**PAGES 18-19**

CHAPTER FIVE Fact and Fiction...**PAGES 20-23**

CHAPTER SIX Bat Conservation...**PAGES 24-29**

Glossary..**PAGE 30**

Suggested Reading, Videos, and Web Sites ....**PAGE 31**

Index ....**PAGE 32**

Chapter One

Bat Basics

What is a bat?

How big are vampire bats?

Read on to learn these answers and more.

What are bats?

Bats are **mammals**, but they are very unique mammals because the bat is the only mammal in the world that can actually fly; flying squirrels only glide. Because bats are so unique, **scientists** have placed them into their own order, or category, called **chiroptera**. Chiroptera is a Latin word that in English literally means hand-wing. This is because the wing of the bat is very similar to a human hand. A bat has four fingers and a thumb with a flight membrane stretched between the fingers. The biggest difference between a human hand and a bat's wing is that the bat's fingers are very long.

▲ BATS HAVE WINGS THAT ARE VERY SIMILAR TO HUMAN HANDS.

How many different types of bats are there?

There are about 1,000 different types of bats. They are separated into two groups: the **megabats** and the **microbats**. In general, megabats are usually larger bats, with large eyes, small ears, and dog-like faces. Megabats live only in places like Africa, Austrailia, and Southeast Asia. Microbats, in general, are usually smaller bats. Most have smaller eyes than megabats, larger ears, and are found throughout the world.

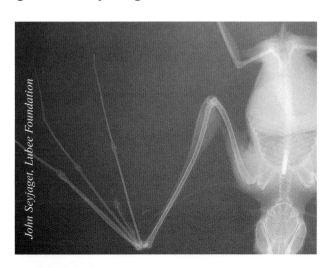

◀

THIS X-RAY SHOWS THE FINGERS OF A BAT'S WING.

Kim Williams

▲ SHOWN HERE IS A
MEXICAN FREE-TAILED BAT.

THE NEARLY 1,000 DIFFERENT
KINDS OF BATS APPEAR IN MANY
SHAPES, SIZES, AND COLORS.

Are there any places where bats don't live?

Yes, there are no bats in the Antarctic where it is too cold. You will also not find bats in extreme hot, dry desert areas where it is too hot.

How big are vampire bats?

Vampire bats are actually quite small. Their body is about 1.18-1.58 cm (3-4 inches) long and their wingspan is about 4.72 cm (12 inches).

Can vampire bats see?

Yes, they have fairly good eyesight.

SHOWN HERE IS A SPECTACLED FLYING FOX. ▶

VAMPIRE BATS ARE ▶
VERY SMALL BATS
WITH A WINGSPAN
OF ONLY ABOUT
12 INCHES. LOOK AT
THE SIZE OF THE BAT
COMPARED TO THE
SIZE OF A DAISY.

ALL MAMMALS,
INCLUDING THIS
BIG BROWN BAT,
HAVE TEETH.
▼

How many kinds of vampire bats are there?

There are three kinds, or species, of vampire bats. The common vampire bat is the most common of the three; they will drink the blood of both mammals and birds. The white-winged vampire bat is rare and drinks the blood of birds and mammals, but seems to prefer bird blood. The hairy-legged vampire bat is the rarest of the three and drinks blood from birds.

7

▲ THERE ARE THREE KINDS OF VAMPIRE BATS. SHOWN HERE IS THE COMMON VAMPIRE BAT.

How many teeth do vampire bats have?

Vampire bats have the fewest number of teeth of all the different kinds of bats. The common vampire bat has only 20 teeth.

How long do vampire bats live?

They can live to be roughly 20 years old.

Do vampire bats have families?

Yes, the common vampire bat lives in *colonies* consisting of relatives and non-relatives.

Are vampire bats nocturnal?

Yes, like most bats, vampire bats become active at night.

Kim Williams

▲
MOST BATS ARE SOCIAL, PREFERRING TO LIVE IN FAMILY GROUPS. SHOWN HERE IS A COLONY OF LITTLE RED FLYING FOXES FROM AUSTRALIA.

Rob Mies

◄
VAMPIRE BATS ARE NOCTURNAL, MEANING THEY BECOME ACTIVE AT NIGHT.

9

Chapter Two

Eating Habits of Vampire Bats

Do vampire bats really drink blood?

How do vampire bats find their food?

Read on to learn these answers and more.

Do vampire bats really drink blood?

Yes, vampire bats are considered obligatory blood feeders. That means they eat nothing else but blood.

Do they drink blood from people?

Occasionally they do drink human blood, but in general they do not like the taste of it.

▲
VAMPIRE BATS FEED ONLY ON BLOOD.

What types of animals do vampire bats drink blood from?

Many years ago, when more *tropical rainforests* were still around, the bats drank blood from *native* animals. Now, because so many native animals have disappeared from rainforest destruction, many of the bats are forced to drink the blood of livestock, like chickens, goats, cows, pigs, and horses.

Does the animal die after the vampire bat drinks from it?

No, the animal doesn't die after a vampire bat has fed off of it. Usually, as the vampire bat is drinking the blood, the animal doesn't even wake up. It may sleep through the whole thing.

▲
SOME BATS EAT INSECTS…

MANY ▶
TYPES
OF BATS
EAT
FRUIT.

OR DRINK NECTAR.
▼

What other types of food do bats eat?

Although the three species of vampire bats only drink blood, there are nearly 1,000 kinds of bats world-wide. Some other things bats eat include fruit, nectar, insects, fish, spiders, and centipedes.

VAMPIRE ▶ BATS DRINK ONLY A SMALL AMOUNT OF BLOOD FROM THEIR PREY.

How do vampire bats find their food?

Because the vampire bat is specially adapted to drink blood, it has very unique ways of finding animals to feed on. It mostly uses its hearing to find food. The vampire bat has, in its brain, a specialized area for detecting the breathing sounds of a sleeping animal. This clues the bat in to where the animal is sleeping. A nightly foraging may go like this: A vampire bat leaves its **roost** looking for a meal. It hears a sleeping animal and lands a few feet away. The common vampire bat is very agile, and sometimes "tiptoes" up to the animal so that it doesn't wake it up. It then uses a special heat-sensory nerve on its nose to find just the right spot to make the tiny incision. This nerve enables the bat to locate the area on the animal where the blood flows close to the skin. It uses its front teeth, which are very sharp, to make that cut. Then it laps up (it doesn't suck blood, but licks it) about two tablespoons of blood.

13

Kim Williams

◀

VAMPIRE BATS USUALLY DRINK THE BLOOD OF LIVESTOCK, LIKE COWS.

How much blood does a vampire bat drink?

Usually only 1 or 2 tablespoons worth. Remember, they are very small, so they do not eat too much.

How does the blood keep flowing as the bat is drinking?

Vampire bats have a special *anticoagulant* in their saliva. This makes sure the blood doesn't clot while the bat is feeding, After the bat leaves, the blood then quickly coagulates. This anticoagulant has been used to help heart patients.

Doctors have made vampire bat saliva into a drug called Draculin. They then give it to people who have problems with their heart.

Kim Williams

◀

A VAMPIRE BAT HAS VERY SPECIAL ADAPTATIONS TO ALLOW IT TO FEED EXCLUSIVELY ON BLOOD. ONE OF THESE ADAPTATIONS IS AN ANTICOAGULANT FOUND IN THEIR SALIVA. THIS ANTICOAGULANT HELPS PREVENT THE ANIMAL'S BLOOD FROM CLOTTING AS THE BAT IS FEEDING FROM IT.

How long can a vampire bat live without drinking blood?

Because of the nutritional content of blood, a vampire bat can usually only lives three days without drinking blood.

▲ VAMPIRE BATS USE THEIR MANY SPECIALIZED SENSES TO FIND THEIR FOOD.

What happens if a vampire bat doesn't get enough food one night?

Vampire bats are very social animals. If one doesn't get enough food it will find a "friend" in the colony. The friend can either be a relative or a non-relative, and is a bat that has shared blood with others before. The hungry bat then begs a blood meal from his friend. The friend bat regurgitates some of the blood into the hungry bat's mouth. This way hardly any bats in the colony starve. The next time the tables may be turned and the friend bat may have not eaten, so he can expect others to share a blood meal with him.

◀ VAMPIRE BATS NEED TO FEED OFTEN. OTHERWISE THEY MAY STARVE TO DEATH. MANY TIMES THEY WILL SHARE A BLOOD MEAL WITH ANOTHER VAMPIRE BAT IN THEIR COLONY.

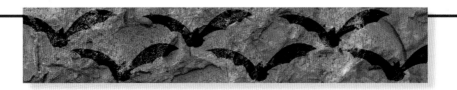

Chapter Three

Habitats of Vampire Bats

Where do vampire bats live?

Where do vampire bats roost?

Read on to learn these answers and more.

Where do vampire bats live?

Many people think that vampire bats live in the United States, but they do not. The only places these bats live are in Central and South America and in Southern Mexico.

▲ VAMPIRE BATS CAN BE FOUND ROOSTING IN CAVES.

SOUTHERN MEXICO

CENTRAL AMERICA

SOUTH AMERICA

Where do vampire bats like to roost?

Vampire bats roost in hollows of trees, in buildings, and in caves.

17

Chapter Four

Baby Vampire Bats

How many babies do vampire bats have?

Do baby vampire bats drink blood?

Read on to learn these answers and more.

How long are mom vampire bats pregnant until they have their babies?

Female vampire bats are pregnant for about 7½ months.

How many babies do vampire bat moms have?

The moms usually have only one baby.

Do baby vampire bats drink blood, too?

At first, baby vampire bats drink milk from their mothers. As they get older, the moms bring back mouthfuls of blood for their babies to taste. At about 24 weeks of age, the babies are on a full blood diet.

LIKE ALL MAMMALS, BABY BATS DRINK MILK FROM THEIR MOTHERS UNTIL THEY ARE OLD ENOUGH TO FIND FOOD ON THEIR OWN. SHOWN HERE ARE TWO BABY BIG BROWN BATS.

VAMPIRE BATS USUALLY HAVE ONLY ONE BABY PER YEAR.

19

Chapter Five

Fact and Fiction

Do vampire bats turn into Count Dracula?

Do vampire bats really walk on two legs?

Read on to learn these answers and more.

Do all vampire bats have rabies?

No, not all bats have *rabies*. If all bats had rabies, there would be no more bats in the world. Bats cannot carry rabies. Like most other mammals, if they get rabies they die from it. Even though not all bats have rabies, and not even most bats have it (actually less than one-half of one percent of bats tested, test positive), some bats do get rabies. Therefore, it is really important to remember never to touch a bat or any other wild animal because there is always a risk that the animal will have the rabies virus.

Kim Williams

VAMPIRE BATS, LIKE ANY MAMMAL, CAN TRANSMIT RABIES TO OTHER ANIMALS. FARMERS IN MEXICO AND CENTRAL AND SOUTH AMERICA NEED TO MAKE SURE THEIR LIVESTOCK ARE PROPERLY VACCINATED AGAINST THIS DISEASE.

Because vampire bats drink blood, don't they transmit rabies more than other animals?

Yes, just by their nature of feeding, they can either get rabies from the animal they are feeding on, or they can pass rabies to that animal easier than most other mammals. Farmers in areas where vampire bats live need to vaccinate their livestock against this virus.

21

▲

STORIES LIKE DRACULA GIVE
VAMPIRE BATS A BAD REPUTATION.
HOWEVER, BY LEARNING MORE
ABOUT THESE BATS, YOU WILL
REALIZE THEY ARE NOT SCARY
CREATURES AT ALL, BUT ARE
ACTUALLY QUITE TIMID AND SHY.

Do vampire bats really turn into Count Dracula?

No, that is just a story people made up. Actually when Bram Stoker wrote his famous book, *Dracula*, he was so fascinated by vampire bats he included them into his book, making many people needlessly afraid of them.

Can vampire bats really walk on two legs?

Yes, these bats are one of the only bats that can occasionally walk upright. This way they can sort of "tiptoe" up to their prey.

I've heard vampire bats adopt baby bats. Is this true?

Yes, there have been some reports of mother vampire bats adopting an orphaned baby vampire bat in the colony.

MOST VAMPIRE BATS CRAWL UP TO THEIR PREY. HOWEVER, SOME MAY WALK ON THEIR HIND FEET AND TIPTOE UP TO THEIR PREY TO FEED ON IT.
▼

▲
VAMPIRE BATS, LIKE OTHER BATS, ARE VERY GOOD MOTHERS. SHOWN HERE IS A MOTHER FRUIT BAT CRADLING HER YOUNG ONE.

Chapter Six

Bat Conservation

Why are vampire bats important?

Are vampire bats endangered?

Read on to learn these answers and more.

Kim Williams

Why are vampire bats important to have around?

Vampire bats are important for many reasons. First of all, they are part of the environment. They are a natural *predator* in the food chain and fit into the food web. They are part of the *ecosystem*. Second, because of the uniqueness of the vampire bat, many scientists study them in order to help people. For example a special drug, called Draculin, has been made from the vampire bat's saliva. This drug, because it contains an anticoagulant, is used to treat heart patients with clotted arteries. In the future, many more drugs may be developed with help from the vampire bat.

If vampire bats only drink a little blood, and they do not kill the animal, why do people hate them so much?

Many people are needlessly afraid of vampire bats because they read scary stories about them. Therefore, lack of knowledge, myths, and movies really make people afraid of vampire bats.

Rob Mies

Kim Williams

▲ IF PEOPLE WORK HARDER TO LET SOME OF THE TREES IN
◀ TROPICAL RAINFORESTS GROW BACK, THAT WOULD PROVIDE
MORE HABITAT FOR NATIVE ANIMALS. THEREFORE, VAMPIRE
BATS WOULD NOT RELY SO HEAVILY ON LIVESTOCK, LIKE
CATTLE, TO FEED ON.

Are vampire bats endangered?

The common vampire bat is not *endangered*. The hairy-legged and white-winged vampire bats are not endangered, but they are very rare.

Do vampire bats need to be controlled in places where they live?

It depends on who you ask. Farmers in Central and South America and Mexico would probably say yes because the bats feed on their livestock. Other people would say no. If we let the tropical rain-forests regrow, the vampire bats would simply begin to feed off wild animals again. This is a hard question because you can see the farmers' point. They don't want their livestock bothered by vampire bats. However, in defense of the vampire bats, they cannot find enough wild animals to feed on, therefore it forces them to turn to livestock.

Why are other types of bats important?

Bats are important for many reasons. Bats in the tropical rainforest that eat fruit help disperse seeds. As a matter of fact, these fruit bats are the main seed dispersers in areas that humans have clear-cut. Without these bats, many trees in the tropics would take a very long time to grow back. Bats that drink *nectar* are important because they help *pollinate* flowers. Some types of flowers are only, or mostly only, pollinated by bats. If these bats were to disappear, the plants would probably disappear. A good example of a plant pollinated by bats is the Saguaro cactus in the western U.S. Bats in the United States mostly eat insects. They eat hundreds of tons of insects each night. One bat can eat 600 to 1,500 mosquito-sized insects each hour. They eat their full body weight in insects each night. That would be like a 45.4 kg (100 lb.) person eating 50 large pizzas. Without these bats, we would be overrun by pesky bugs. Farmers would be in deep trouble, too. Bats love to munch on insects that eat crops, like grasshoppers, screwworms, and even gypsy moths.

Kim Williams

▲
FRUIT BATS ARE EXTREMELY IMPORTANT FOR THE TROPICAL RAINFORESTS.

John Seyjaget, Lubee Foundation

◀
THEY DISPERSE SEEDS SO THE RAINFOREST TREES CAN EVENTUALLY GROW BACK.

Where can I see bats?

There are many places in the world where you can see bats. Many zoos across the country have great bat displays including the Brookfield Zoo in Illinois, Bronx Zoo in New York, Philadelphia Zoo in Pennsylvania, the Oregon Zoo in Oregon, Woodland Park Zoo in Washington, and the Milwaukee County Zoo in Wisconsin. You can also visit some
of the places listed below:

- The University of Florida Bat House, on Lake Alice on the University of Florida campus, Gainesville, Florida. This large bat house is home to 60,000 Mexican free-tailed bats. You can watch them emerge from the bat house on warm summer evenings.

- The Florida Bat Center in Punta Gorda, Florida. An educational and conservation center for native Florida bats. Live Florida bats are on exhibit and a great gift shop is on the premises. Call 941-637-6990 for hours.

- The Lubee Foundation in Gainesville, Florida. Lubee is an educational facility that houses megabats on its beautiful facility. Teachers and students are always welcome by appointment. Call 352-485-1250 for more information.

- The Organization for Bat Conservation's live bat programs. OBC is leading the way when it comes to educating North America about bat conservation. Researchers travel across the U.S. presenting programs using live bats. Call 1-800-276-7074 to get a list of scheduled presentations in your area.

- Carlsbad Caverns in Carlsbad, New Mexico. During the summer months you can watch roughly 250,000 Mexican free-tailed bats emerge at dusk from a natural amphitheater. Call 505-785-2232 for more information.

- Bat World Sanctuary and Living Museum in Mineral Wells, Texas. The sanctuary offers educational programs and has many types of bats to view. You can see Bat World by appointment only, call 817-325-3404.

What is The Organization for Bat Conservation?

OBC is a non-profit organization that saves bats. It is leading the way in bat conservation education. Projects include ecological research, like surveys, to help protect bats and their habitats. Conservation programs, like seminars to land owners, government agencies, and the media, are geared directly toward saving bats. OBC also tests bat houses as alternative roosts for bats. These bat houses give bats a place to live, and because most of the bats' natural habitat is destroyed, they really need it! Most importantly, OBC presents hundreds of educational programs every year on the benefits, misunderstandings, and uniqueness of bats. Since 1990, thousands of programs have been given to schools, nature centers, stores, zoos, parks, museums, and other interested groups and clubs. Programs are an interactive adventure into the fascinating world of bats, consisting of a slide presentation, a discussion of how to protect bats, and a look at some live bats.

Wow! A group dedicated to saving bats! How can I join?

We strongly urge you to join in OBC's fight to save bats. Memberships are $25 and up and benefits include the quarterly *"Bat Conservation Journal"*, in-formation about bats specific to your state, a catalog, and other great stuff. Please check out their website at www.batconservation.org or call 1-800-276-7074 for more information.

JOINING AN ORGANIZATION THAT WORKS ▶ TO PROTECT BATS IS ONE WAY YOU CAN HELP SAVE THEM.

Glossary

Anticoagulant: A substance that delays or prevents the clotting of blood.

Chiroptera: The order or group bats are in. Literally means hand-wing.

Colony: A group of bats roosting together.

Ecosystem: A system made up of a community of animals, plants, and bacteria living together.

Endangered: A plant or animal that is in danger of becoming extinct.

Mammal: The group of animals that have hair, nurse their babies milk, breathe air, have live birth, and have a backbone.

Megabat: A subgroup of bats. In general, they are large, with large eyes, small ears, and live in the old-world tropics.

Microbat: A subgroup of bats. In general, they are small, with small eyes, large ears, use echolocation, and are found throughout the world.

Native: Belonging to a locality by birth.

Nectar: The sweet liquid in flowers.

Pollinate: The process of bringing pollen to one plant from another, thereby increasing genetic diversity.

Predator: An animal that eats another living thing.

Rabies: A deadly disease that affects the nervous system of mammals.

Roost: A place where bats rest.

Scientist: A specialist in science.

Tropical rainforest: An area of lush vegetation and a large amount of rainfall.

Suggested Reading and Videos

Books:

"**Understanding Bats**" by Kim Williams and Rob Mies

"**Amazing Bats**" by Eyewitness Junior Series, No. 13

"**Building a Better Bat House**" by The Organization for Bat Conservation

"**Stella Luna**" by Janell Cannon

"**Zipping, Zapping, Zooming Bats**" A stage 2 "Let's-read-and-find-out" science book.

Videos:

"**Bats—The True Story**". A 30-minute video giving you all the bat information you could possibly want in an easy-to-understand context. This is the best, and most up-to-date video on the market, with wonderful footage of live bats.

Posters:

"**Bats of the Eastern United States**" Poster measures 20 x 28 inches and is available for $10 (includes tax & shipping).

"**Bats of the Western United States**" Poster measures 20 x 28 inches and is available for $10 (includes tax & shipping).

If you are interested in any of these items, you can get them through The Organization for Bat Conservation www.batconservation.org

Adopt-a-bat programs:

The Organization for Bat Conservation offers a wonderful Adopt-a-bat program. You can adopt a bat of your choice to help with medical and feeding expenses. Sponsors receive a poster (one of the above), a letter of thanks from their bat, and information about their bat with a photo. Contact OBC for a list of bats to adopt.

Web Sites:

The Organization for Bat Conservation **www.batconservation.org**

Basically Bats **www.lads.com/bbi/index.html**

Florida Bat Center **www.floridabats.org**

The Lubee Foundation **www.lubee.com**

Buzbee Bat House **www.batbox.org**

The Backyard Bat Page **http://web-it.com/bats/**

The Bat Conservation Trust **www.bats.org.uk/default.htm**

Bat Conservation Society of Canada **www.cancaver.ca/bats/canada.htm**

AUSTROP (in Austrailia) **www.austrop.org.au/**

Philadelphia Zoo **www.phillyzoo.org/pz0124.htm**

Ranger Rick Bat Page **www.nwf.org/nwf/rrick/batbs96.html**

Carslbad Caverns **www.carlsbad.caverns.national park.com/**

Warwickshire Bat Group **www.jwaller.demon.co.uk/batgroup/**

Bat House Discussion Group **http://home.paclink.com/~davem/ data/dgroups/bats/**

Hope Canyon **www.hopecanyon.org**

London Bat Group **www.cixco.uk/~pguest/bg/lbg.html**

The Bat Cave **www2.torstar.com/rom/batcave/**

Ruwenzori Fruit Bats At Zoo Boise **www.sunvalleyski.com/zooboise/ bats.html**

INDEX

Big brown bat, 8, 19
Birth, 19
Brain, 13
Chiroptera, 5
Common
vampire bat, 8, 13
Count Dracula, 22
Draculin, 14, 25
Fruit bat, 11, 23, 27

Hairy-legged
vampire bat, 8, 26
Heat-sensory nerve, 13
Hoary bat, 6
Importance of, 14, 25, 27
Life expectancy, 8
Little red flying fox, 9
Megabats, 5

Mexican
free-tailed bat, 6, 28
Microbats, 5
Myths, 22, 25
Rabies, 21
Roosts, 17
Size, 6-7
Specialized
senses, 13-15

Spectacled flying fox, 6
Teeth, 7, 13
The Organization for
Bat Conservation, 28-29
White-winged
vampire bat, 8, 26
Walking, 23
Wing, 5
Zoos, 28

WE WOULD LIKE TO THANK THE FOLLOWING PEOPLE FOR THEIR ENCOURAGEMENT AND PARTICIPATION:
SUSAN BARNARD, DIRECTOR OF BASICALLY BATS, THE FIRST PHONE CALL I MAKE WHEN I HAVE A
BAT QUESTION; DENISE TOMLINSON, DIRECTOR OF OPERATIONS AT THE ORGANIZATION FOR BAT
CONSERVATION, FOR BEING SUCH A SPECIAL FRIEND AND HELPING ME FIND ANSWERS TO SOME
OF MY QUESTIONS; JOHN SEYJAGET, DIRECTOR OF THE LUBEE FOUNDATION FOR DONATING SUCH
GREAT SLIDES AND CARL SAMS AND JEAN STOICK OF CARL SAMS PHOTOGRAPHY
FOR ALL THE YEARS OF FRIENDSHIP AND SUPPORT.